Know Your Purpose

A Practical Guide to Living your Life on Purpose

Min. Harrell L. Henton

Acknowledgements

Special thanks to my heavenly Father for His Grace and Mercy that has kept me all my days.

Thanks to my family for your invaluable support, inspiration, prayers, encouragement, and continuous wisdom. To my Brownsville Church of Christ family, I love you and thank you for your prayers over this endeavor.

To my beautiful wife Kellee, my son Harrison, and my daughter Kaleah, I thank you for all your sacrifices that you have made so that God may use me for His purpose. I love you!!

About the Author

Minister Harrell L. Henton has been working for the Lord for as long as he can remember. Under the guidance of his grandfather, Robert L. Holt Sr., he has made the grand decision to dedicate his full life to the work of the Lord and His church. Born on July 6, 1983, he is the third of four children born to Leroy and Hester Henton. He is a graduate of Miami Carol City Senior High and after finishing there, he matriculated to Florida Memorial University, where he studied Communications. Beginning his path toward the work of the church, Harrell became a Christian, after being baptized into the body of Christ, on January 10, 1993, at the tender age of 9. From there, Harrell continued to spend time with his grandfather and mentor, Robert Holt Sr., a minister of a small, robust congregation in Miami, Florida. Harrell began to learn an abundance about the word of God, words of wisdom, and just in general learning more about becoming a man. Little did he know at the time that he was being groomed to one day take over the ministry of the Brownsville Church of Christ. In August of 2011, Harrell, was handed the torch to deliver God's word. He was installed as the full-time minister of the Brownsville Church of Christ on August 22, 2011. From there, he decided to make it his mission to continue to build the Brownsville congregation as a loving and family-oriented church. With the support and encouragement of his family and membership, he has begun to build this church, increasing membership, creating more programs, and strengthening the programs already in existence.

As a young man leading a great church, many times it can be difficult, but Minister Henton understands that success does not come without hard work, but he knows that with God all things are possible! Although Bro. Henton had his plate full of a full-time ministry position and working a full-time job outside of the ministry, he still found the time to find his helpmate. He began dating the former Kellee L. Pratt in September 2008. It perhaps was a little tough over the years considering they had a long-distance relationship, but through God all things are possible. They made it work and three years later in December 2011, they made it official by tying the knot. Being married for nine years, Harrell and Kellee

Henton have two beautiful children, Harrison and Kaleah. Harrell has his plate full. However, he is up for the challenge. Having a close relationship with the Lord and living by the Word of God, he knows that he will be blessed, no matter what the situation is. Currently, Minister Henton is a certified Chaplain, ordained Pastor, approved pre-marital/ post – marital counselor, sought after mentor, public speaker and self-published author of The Wisdom Journey. Min. Henton's written encouragement happens to be one of his favorite scriptures, "Trust in the Lord with all thine heart; and lean not unto thine own understanding, in all thy ways acknowledge Him and He shall direct thy path (Proverbs 3:5-6).

Table of Contents

Prologue

The greatest accomplishment that we can attain is to believe in ourselves. This is the greatest, in my opinion because it allows you to operate with a sense of hope, strength, and even courage. If you believe in yourself, you have overcome the obstacle that most people struggle with which is self-denial. The reason many individuals struggle in this capacity is primarily because they have allowed themselves to digest the image that the world around them has defined as being beautiful, blessed or someone of importance. When we look at television, or listen to the radio, we are given an image of what success looks like and what will those around us supposedly will accept. Therefore, if we are not content within our own selves, we would perpetually change our image to fit the image of what has been defined as acceptable.

Take a second to imagine all the various images that we are exposed to daily that are streamed to us through the news, social media, talk radio, and the music that we listen to. We are shown that sex sells, and if you are not sexy then you will not be accepted. According to Statista.com, in the United States the entertainment and media market was worth an estimated 678 billion U.S. dollars in 2018 and was expected to grow to 720 billion U.S. dollars by 2020. As Americans, we literally have consumed entertainment as our drug of choice when we want to see or hear about how we need to live our lives. Many people have begun to define their lives based upon the latest trends, craze, or fads which is any form of collective behaviors that develops within a culture, generation, or social group in which a group of people follow as impulse for a finite period. I recall when I was twelve years old and in the middle of learning about life along with the "birds & bees" that I noticed how fashion changed constantly. At that time there was a cultural shift that was happening amongst my friends regarding our haircuts and the unspoken rule to no longer ask for a "part" when getting a haircut. Before this time, we were telling our barbers to give us "parts" and designs in our head like the rappers were getting. We would ask for numbers, symbols, and designs that we believed would allow us to be accepted amongst our peers or make us look cool. However, there was a shift whereas everyone stopped getting designs and lines in their heads because someone famous said that it was now "out of style". The hairstyle now for guys had transitioned to having a low haircut with waves, or a small afro like the rapper, the late Craig Mack.

When I realized the change, I changed because I did not want to do what I liked, but I wanted to do what others liked. This happens every day to a lot of women and men within our society today. For example, they change their appearance to the way that is accepted by their friends and foes. Therefore, in the pursuit of attempting to fit in or be accepted, it will steadily cause a person to lose themselves trying to be someone else. When we really think about it, do we really know who we are? Or to whom we are? Although I believe we are shaped by our world and those things that we experience, I genuinely believe that we must still find out our own identity. One of the greatest philosophers to ever live, Mahatma Gandhi sought to achieve self-realization. He stated, "What I want to achieve – what I have been striving and pining to achieve – is self-realization..." (Gandhi, 1940). Self-realization is equally truth-realization. We should aspire to find and become our true selves so that the world may see the mighty blessing that flows through us genuinely. God made you the way that you are for His purpose, and His glory! We must remember that every tooth, hair follicle, fingernail, and body part was made specifically for you and no one else. The bible says in Ephesians 2:10, "For we are His workmanship, created in Christ Jesus unto good works, which God hath before ordained that we should walk in them."

Chapter 1:

Smile for the Camera

This expression means to look with a kindly or amused expression, to look derisively at instead of being annoyed. This expression which is often used by those that are taking pictures or recording a video. Furthermore, this expression or phrase is used to encourage those that are looking sad or frowning for a picture. It is said to encourage the person that is being photographed and/ or recorded to bring joy and happiness into the space at that time. This is remarkably interesting because it encourages a person to display an external gesture that they may not be feeling the same internally. I have learned that it can be dangerous to display a false reality to those around us because of the perception that may be perceived by them if you show them your "true colors." Therefore, we must never allow another person or persons to determine how we carry and present ourselves because of fear of being excluded and not accepted. When I look at social media these days, I see the evidence of people endeavoring to show the best side of themselves so that any observer will see something flawless, perfect, and beautiful. Consider how many clicks of the camera it took for someone to post a picture of themselves with the heading, "I woke up like this..."

We live in a society that has perpetuated the idea that beauty is forever, and that blemishes are not natural, so never show them! We are fed through our entertainment and electronic devices that if we are not smiling then that cannot be beauty, or it is not sexy. The expectation to be beautiful all the time can be difficult, and we must understand that God has made us all unique for His purpose. Personally, because of my position as a Pastor, I have always felt like I was held to a standard whereas I have to "smile" or be mistake-free all the time. Furthermore, I have sometimes felt like there were eyes on me to make sure that I do everything correctly from praying to preaching. For example, there has been times when I missed a word, mistakenly overlooked a member, or did not say everyone's name in a prayer... someone would attempt to always correct me. So, the pressure to be perfect seemed to be engulfing for me, which caused me to occasionally get into a state of falling into depression and at times being introverted. I felt like the expectations for me were so high that I begin to feel like giving up on life and literally taking my life because I cared about how others perceived me. Since I knew that I would not be able to fulfill their expectations consistently, I would just end my life so that I do not have to worry about disappointing anyone, anymore. Life can be difficult if you are constantly adjusting yourself to satisfy the standards of others because of the expectations that they have for you. We must realize that we will never accomplish the standards that others have set for us, primarily because the standards are always changing making it difficult to obtain.

Consider the fact that we live in a society that changes its "mind" quiet often and very quickly. According to U.S. News and World Report who pulled a report from Pew Research Center study, 14 percent of Americans have changed their views on a political or social topic in the last year because of something they saw on social media. Furthermore, the report stated that only 6 percent of those aged 65 and older said their views changed because of social media, compared to 23 percent of those aged 18 to 29.

Those aged 30 to 49 and 50 to 64 years of age were almost equally as likely – 14 percent compared to 13 percent, respectively. Men were far more likely than woman to change their minds because of something they saw on social media. Forty-one percent of men compared to just 29 percent of women reported having their views changed. According to the report, it was most common among younger men, with 29 percent of those aged 18 to 29 changing their opinions, compared to only 12 percent of men 30 and older. It is interesting to know that we change our minds, opinions, and thoughts about something or someone so frequently. So, to become someone that dictates their life of what people say or think will cause you to never know who you really are. In the words of Denis Waitley, an American writer, "A smile is the light in your window that tells others that there is a caring, sharing person inside." Smile because you want to, and not because you must...know that it is through your uniqueness that God intended for you to bless the world!

Chapter 2:

Finding Myself

Who am I? What is it that I am called to do, or become? I believe that these questions are the most perplexing questions to answer because they must deal with our purpose. Many of us struggle to find our purpose in life, and we have a hard time articulating who we are to people because we really do not know who we are ourselves. Your purpose is the thing that you do the absolute best with the least amount of effort from the standpoint of skills and abilities. If you bake cookies better than anyone you know, you should be somewhere baking cookies. There are people that have made millions of dollars baking cookies and selling them. If you wake up in a rut because you must go to a job that you do not love, or regret having to clock-in at your place of employment, then you are not moving in your purpose. You do not want to live your whole life and not walk in the purpose that God has called you to walk in. Yes, God has called all of us to having a purpose-driven life, but we do not always answer the call. In fact, we do not even allow ourselves to answer the proverbial telephone when God calls us to our gift and/ or purpose. It has been said that the consequences of not finding your life purpose include chronic, lingering dissatisfaction which is an absence of inner peace and a sense of not being fully in sync with your inner self.

There are people throughout this world that are unable to articulate what they are here for, but they are on a search to find that "certain something" that defines and integrates their lives. Many people turn to various books and to many programs to help them to find their life's purpose, but they still have not found what they are looking for. That is because your true inner self knows that your life purpose is out of sync with your outer actions. In a conversation with one of my mentors and great scholars, Dr. Freeman T. Wyche, he stated that "Every being is intended to be on earth for a certain purpose." Additionally, he told me that "No one can do what God has put you here to do", which means that each of us are on earth to fulfill a specific task set by God aforetime. So, the question that a lot of us find extremely hard to answer, and that a great number of people struggle with is their reason for being. We sometimes struggle with trying to find out, what is the reason I am here on earth, and how do I find out what that truly is? I recently attended a funeral of a young woman that had recently became a mother, wife, and at that time was hired as a mental health therapist. This young lady was always on a pursuit to find out what was the meaning of her life, and how she would make an impact on this world. She had recently graduated from a prestigious university obtaining her master's degree in Psychology. Before her death, she stated to me that she had many plans to become a great person in her community, and throughout the world by helping those that are hurting. She made plans for years, but she never was able to fulfill her purpose because her life was cut short due to a brain aneurysm. Many of us have goals, aspirations, and sometimes dreams but do we ever set out to accomplish them? We talk about how we want to be business owners or create the next invention, but because of FEAR we never make our dreams a reality.

How then do I find myself? The way that you can find out who you are is to look within yourself and write down three things that you would enjoy doing without being paid for it. I believe that we all have something that we would love to do, but we are fearful of failing, fearful of not being heard, fearful of not making enough money to survive. The bible reminds us in Proverbs 16:9 (ESV), "The heart of man plans his way, but the Lord establishes his steps." This scripture reminds us that we must first make plans in the arena of what we love to do, and then God will give us the direction to our destiny. According to the University of Scranton, 92 percent of people who set New Year's goals never actually achieve them. As a result, only 8 percent of people are achieving their goals in life, they are called goal-achievers. It can be scary to make a move into your purpose because it is not always a clear-cut plan on how to become what God has called you to be. So, when you begin to write down those three things that you enjoy doing the most, then begin to move forward with reading, studying, and seeking out resources that will help you to achieve your purpose in life. Les Brown, the great American motivational speaker says, "Too many of us are not living our dreams because we are living our fears." Begin to investigate how you can achieve your true purpose in life by taking time throughout the day to invest in your dream and your reason for living.

This pursuit of happiness has oftentimes been difficult to obtain but the key in finding it is to never quit. There are many people that have settled even though they were just inches away from becoming what God has called them to be. Therefore, you must continue to pursue your happiness, and to find out what is the impact you will make on this world. Dr. Martin Luther King Jr. stated, "If a man is called to be a street sweeper, he should sweep streets even as Michelangelo painted, or Beethoven composed music, or Shakespeare wrote poetry. He should sweep streets so well that all the hosts of heaven and earth will pause to say, here lived a great street sweeper who did his job well." Whatever your purpose is, do it with all the might and strength that you have believing that this is what God has called you to do while you lived. So, today take time to look at yourself in the mirror and speak words of affirmation to yourself with the result becoming actionable steps that will cause you to meet your goals. By doing these things, I believe that you will begin to live out your purpose, and people will finally meet the true you for the first time.

Chapter 3:

I am U.G.L.Y
(UNIQUE, GIFTED, LOVED, YOUTHFUL)

It is funny to me to know that that there is a definition for the word **ugly**, which is universally accepted. According to dictionary.com, the definition for the adjective **ugly** means to be very unattractive or unpleasant to look at. Also, it states that the word **ugly** means to be offensive to the sense of beauty or displeasing in appearance; disagreeable. Therefore, we are all given the liberty to define what we deem to be **ugly** or beautiful every day. The fact that something is unattractive says that there is another end of the spectrum which is deemed to be attractive. Growing up in elementary school, that was something that I dealt with amongst my peers because those around me were overly critical about my physical looks. I was occasionally laughed at and spoken negatively about because of my big lips. In retrospect, it was amazing to know that children can be very mean at times to each other over the way a person looks. It was truly a tough time for me in my life during elementary school because I was not embraced as the most attractive kid, or the one that drew the attention of girls. Although I was occasionally scrutinized for my looks by others, introspectively I felt that I was a good-looking boy and that I was blessed. My mother was very integral for me because although I went to school and was laughed at, when I got home, I was loved and encouraged. I was told by my parents that I was strong, handsome, blessed, and loved daily. Consequently, I was able to endure the mean kids during my elementary time because my parents continued to instill in me that I was not **ugly**, but I was unique, gifted, loved, and youthful. I genuinely believe that affirmation from those that you love is especially important, or from those that you regard as important so that you can develop a healthy sense of self-worth. Self-worth is the deep, unshakable belief that someone has that they are loved and worthy to be loved. Individuals with high self-worth tend to have higher respect, confidence, and values. Individuals with low self-worth might suffer from low confidence and feel bad about themselves.

You are unique! There is something about you that is great, and that allows you to be idiosyncratic amongst a changing society. The question is what makes you unique? We are unique because we could only fulfill something that no one else can do except for us. Our uniqueness is particularly important because we are made to do a specific thing while we are living on this time side of life. The word unique means being the only one of its kind; unlike anything else. You must believe that you are unique meaning that you have something that is unexplainable, but especially important to display so that the world may see. Many times, people will not understand the things that make you who you are primarily because it is not their ideal of what is normal or cool. For example, some people are very eclectic when it comes to the way that they dress daily. They may enjoy wearing boots with a dress, a sweater with short pants, or a lime green t-shirt with red sweatpants. The point is that we all have a uniqueness about us that we must exhibit, so that there can be diversity and not uniformity.

Dr. Paul Bloom, a professor of psychology at Yale University and author of the book, How Pleasure Works: The New Science of Why We Like What We Like, states that when we get pleasure that it is not based upon what we see or hear. Rather it is based upon what we believe the thing that gives us pleasure to be. For example, when we listen to a song by one of our favorite music artists, we seem to be more willing to like the song whereas if it was a song by a street performer that no one has heard of. Furthermore, he concludes that wine does not taste as good if you do not know it is expensive or a special wine from a great collection. A painting is going to look different to you, and you are going to value it differently, depending on who you think created it. Dr. Bloom states that when you look at a painting, you do not just look at the patterns of color and the shapes and the perceptual input. Rather, you try to reconstruct what went on during its creation. What is the history? What is its real nature? And that determines how much you like it. The conclusion regarding this series of thinking is to help us to realize that we all look at and do things differently which helps us too inevitably not be exactly alike. Think about what makes you unique from those individuals that you spend time around, or the people that you see throughout the day. You are special, you are one-of-a- kind and there is greatness within you that is awaiting to be seen through you.

You are Gifted! To say that you are gifted, that means that you are exceptional, remarkable, and talented. Do you remember in school the separation of gifted students and regular students? The elementary school that I attended as a little kid bused the gifted students to another school for advanced learning. Although I was not considered gifted at an early age by those that grade IQ test and make recommendations, within my own mind I believed that I was remarkable. I did not always get the "A" or made the Honor Roll every semester, but I still carried myself with dignity and self-assurance. I strongly believed that those that were gifted were very smart and knew how to solve problems very quickly and accurately. Nevertheless, being gifted should not be measured solely on those parameters because it will exclude those that have extraordinary abilities in other areas of life. Do you believe that you are gifted? What area(s) of life are you gifted in? Never allow a test or a document to define your ability to cause you to think that you cannot affect change in this world. Intellectual ability is something to be proud of, if you have it, but there are other abilities that others have been endowed with that has made a great impact on our world.

According to forbes.com (2017), just 23 of America's 400 richest people have high school degrees and 2 dropped out of high school without ever going to college. According to businessinsider.com, Jay-Z, first hip-hop billionaire, never graduated from high school. Although he publicly encourages people to value education and consider it important for their success. Again, there are numerous people that are gifted in areas separate of academics, such as sports, music, building, drawing, dance, and/ or leadership. There are things that we all can do to display the degree of being gifted everyday if we simply believe. After you believe in yourself, then begin to work on your area of gifted so that it may be helpful to everyone. If you are a gifted athlete, invest in your wellness and technique so that you can be the best athlete that you can be! If you are a gifted dancer, take time to perfect your craft and skills that will allow you to be amongst great dancers! If you are gifted in leadership, you must continue to develop your interpersonal and communication skills so that you can lead a team effectively. Whatever area(s) you are gifted in, continue to work on the intangibles in those areas because you may be the greatest to ever do what it is that you do.

You are Loved! Love can come in many shapes and sizes. It is through love that we can recognize the extent of how much someone cares or considers another person. Love, throughout scripture has been defined as patient, kind, not self-seeking, not easily angered, not boastful, but rejoices with the truth. Love can have a strong effect on those that are recipients of it if the person would truly embrace it. The reason why I say that an individual must embrace it, because many individuals have been hurt under the theme of love. Therefore, love is not always accepted so easily, it must prove to be genuine. As I have mentioned earlier, my parents consistently showed me love and never allowed me to feel like I was not important even though my peers did not. One of my favorite songwriters and R&B singers, Musiq Soulchild states in a song that, "many people use loves' name in vain and that those that have faith in love sometimes go astray." Even though love may not have been favorable to you, you can still love yourself with all your mind, body, and soul. Sometimes we are looking for love from people that are not trying to love us back, in fact they may be having a hard time loving themselves. As a result, you must love yourself by smiling more, writing down a few things that you love about yourself, and treating yourself to moments of self-care.

As a preacher of the gospel of Jesus Christ, I have oftentimes preached about love along with its importance to the well-being of mankind. Biblically, you can read that love is the reason that Jesus came down to earth and died on the old, rugged cross. The bible states in John 3:16, "God so loved the world that He gave His only begotten Son, that whosoever believeth in Him should not perish, but have everlasting life." It was because of love that God sent His Son Jesus to sacrifice His life so that those that believe upon Him may be saved from eternal damnation.

Therefore, you must remember that you are loved by God, which is a love that is good enough. God loves you, and there is nothing that you can do about it! Some people may be perplexed about the love of God because their definition of love is through conditions and clauses. However, God's love is unconditional meaning that God's love is extended toward us without any "strings" attached to it. This type of love is used within the Christian faith is called Agape. Agape, a Greek word that is often translated "love" in the New Testament is used to describe the love that is and from God, whose nature is love itself. Agape love does not come naturally to us, we must be led by the Holy Spirit that will give us guidance on how to love those that are unlovable. As a child, I used to sing a song that reminded us that Jesus loves the little children and that they are precious in His sight. That song although quite simple, was very inspiring because its purpose was to remind children that they are loved by Jesus, the Son of God. Remember that you are loved by God, and that you are special in His sight!

The other day I was at a homeless shelter ministering to both men and women about the power of God. During my conversations, I realized that many of them were missing the love that comes from God that would allow them to start loving themselves again. Many of them had concluded that their families, friends, and children all hated them and at some point, they started believing that they should be hated. I found this to be remarkably interesting that they began to believe that they were insignificant primarily because the people close to them believed it about them. If we are not careful, we can believe the same thing about ourselves because those closest to us believe that we are insignificant. The reason why those at the homeless shelter, and even some of us will began to believe this untruth is because we have allowed ourselves to be defined by what others say about us. My friend, you must remember that God loves you, and that you are somebody in His Eyes, and that He died on the cross for you because He loves you. God loves you just the way that you are, and when He made you, He said in His Word that you were good! It is not uncommon to sometimes forget that you are loved because there is so much negativity in our world, and propaganda that we hear daily. Nevertheless, remember that you are loved and therefore make sure that you love yourself regardless of if no one else loves you.

You are Youthful! Someone once said that age is nothing but a number. Whether this is true or not, you are blessed if you enjoy life to the fullest and take care of yourself. Therefore, whatever age you are is a blessing because we do not know what tomorrow will bring, and if we will live to see tomorrow.

Since I entered ministry, I have attended over 100 funerals of people ranging from newborn babies to a one-hundred-year-old matriarch. Knowing this, it is imperative that you be youthful, which is to have vitality or freshness of youth. So, as you go throughout your day today, do something that will express your youthfulness such as taking a walk in the cool breeze, dance to your favorite song on the radio, or do something spontaneous this evening. Whatever you decide, have fun while doing it and do not worry about tomorrow. I recall when I was a boy, I would be worry-free walking to the park to play with my friends and just live in the moment. As an adult, that can be a little difficult especially if you have a family, but I want to encourage you to seek out opportunities to be youthful, and to live in the moment. Have fun, smile, laugh, dance, play a game, or climb a tree! According to everydaypower.com (September 2020), many people do not take risk because either we do not think we are good enough or we do not think we will be loved the same way or loved enough.

Simply, we spend too much time listening to our own doubts and the doubts of others. We have perhaps spent too much time focusing on the obstacles rather than the goals. We spend too much time judging, evaluating, and attempting to be in control so much that we cannot get out of our own head or out of our own way. Also, we are afraid that by making certain decisions we will lose the approval of the people closest to us. Furthermore, this article stated that we become people pleasers and lose our sense of purpose in the process. We think that if we do certain things that our family, friends, coworkers will become disconnected or even think we are crazy. On the other hand, we must know that although some may be unimpressed, others will be inspired by your ability to live out your passion with confidence and fortitude without being afraid of taking risk. According to Mahatma Gandhi, "Your life is your message, make it an inspiring one!" Therefore, live your life as an example of someone who will not settle for less than what you are or what you are destined to be. Be youthful and full of vigor so that you can conquer all the things that you have been thinking about, but never had the courage to attempt.

Youthfulness permits us to be expressive in ways that keeps us energetic so that we can conquer the world. Your energy and excitement are truly something that will benefit you as you dive into your purpose in life. Consider how children are so agile on the playground, meaning to move quickly and easily without any feelings of restraint. They have the courage to climb to the highest point of the playground equipment without difficulty and then they jump down like a predator launching upon their prey without hesitation. Have you ever watched as children explore mother nature when they go outside of their home, or at a park? They pick up tree limbs, jump in and out of bushes, run up and down the sidewalk in front of the houses in the neighborhood. Children teach us to explore our environment without fear or hesitation because it can limit us from having a happier, and more adventurous life that would lead us to our greater selves. Regardless of whatever age you are, you can still have vigor and be innovative in your ideas because you have all the tools to show the world that you are youthful. May you live out your destiny and have fun in the process is my prayer for you. Be Youthful!!

Chapter 4:

Look in the Mirror

A mirror is typically made of glass with a flat curvy surface and has a reflective covering over it. Mirrors are not only for appearance; they are also used in technological and scientific components. Before mirrors were manufactured, pools of water were often used to see a reflection. According to Wikipedia.org, a mirror is an object that reflects an image. Light that bounces off a mirror will show an image of whatever is in front of it, when focused through the lens of the eye or a camera. My question to you is, "have you looked in the mirror today?" If you have, you should have seen a person that has great potential but not fulfilled to its total capacity. When you looked in the mirror you should have seen greatness, beauty, resilience, and courage. I believe that you are a person that has been through adversities in life, but you are an overcomer. You are a person that will continue to be great regardless of your circumstances. Some people when they look in the mirror, they see misery, shame, and defeat. I have heard people say that your perception can become your reality, meaning that the lens or mindset you view something will be perceived true by the observer. Therefore, you must think greatness, and not defeat. You must think blessings, and not curses. You must think positively, and not negatively. The former president of the United States of America, the late Lyndon B. Johnson stated, "Yesterday is not ours to recover, but tomorrow is ours to win or lose."

Biblically, King David understood the power of having hope and faith in God in every circumstance. King David approximately wrote 75 Psalms in the Bible, which speak about deliverance, patience, regret, forgiveness, and faith. My favorite Psalm that King David wrote in the Bible is Psalm 40, which begins by saying that he cried unto the Lord and waited patiently for Him. After King David waited for the Lord, He states that the Lord heard his cry and proceeded to strengthen Him and deliver Him from the pit, metaphorically speaking. As a result, King David rejoices in the Lord which allows others to see that God is willing to deliver those that seek His deliverance. King David was remarkably like all of us because He was a man that did not always look at Himself as champion of faith, but through revelations and experiences, he believed. He started believing that He could do the impossible with the help and guidance of the Lord! Just like King David, you must look in the mirror and began to know that God has instilled greatness within you, but you must began today walking in that greatness.

The apostle Paul wrote an epistle to the church at Ephesus in Ephesians 4:1; "I therefore, a prisoner for the Lord, urge you to walk in a manner worthy of the calling to which you have been called, with humility and gentleness, with patience..." So, walk worthy in your calling, and be the best at everything you do because you are great! Also, the mirror reminds us that we are not all the same. It reminds us that we all are created with different features, scars, wrinkles, and perfect imperfections. We must learn how to embrace the way that God has created us, which is in His own image. Whatever way that you perceive your appearance to be, remember that God has made you just the way that pleased Him, so remember that you are good enough! Today, look in the mirror and think about the things that make you unique from everyone else, and write them on a sticky note then put them on the mirror that you look at every day. This will allow you to keep positivity in front of you, and to be reminded daily that you are a blessing made by God for a great purpose!

Chapter 5:

Form & Fill

Throughout the Bible, there has been countless examples of how God was able to guide individuals with the resources that they needed to move into their purpose. God provided the strength, protection, equipment, and even the weapons to allow the person to move into their purpose. Specifically, in Second Kings 4:1 – 7; this story shows us that each of us must participate in the process of a purpose-driven life. Consider this woman that has been preparing for ministry with her husband who is a son of the prophets and is preparing for the calling on His life. As she is preparing to be a prophet's wife, the text indicates that he has died, as a result, the creditors are coming to take her two children as collateral for the debt in which her husband has incurred.

This woman is now in a place where she has become discouraged and disappointed because there is no longer any income coming in the house so that she may survive. She now is in contact with the prophet Elisha, and she tells him that her sons will be taken soon, and that she does not have anything of worth in her house to pay off her husband's debt, except her two children. This woman is now in a place of desperation and despair because it seems like she is headed toward a downward spiral regarding her well-being and security. She has reached a point where she has nowhere to go, but the prophet Elisha asks her, "What does she have in her house?" She indicates to him that all she has is a pot of oil and that is it.

This question is a remarkably interesting one because it caused the widow woman to look within her capacity to see if she has something of value within her home that she was overlooking. It is inferred that she looked at the last jar of oil as an extension of her poverty and not of her purpose. Once Elisha heard about the oil, he instructed her to go to her neighbors and borrow jars and bring them back to her home. As she brought the jars to her home, the scriptures states that God filled them. It was through her ability to obey the command of gathering the jars and to bring them to the place that the prophet Elisha commanded her to bring them that she begins to see the power of God! God begins to fill the jars with oil as the widow presents jars before Him. There is without a doubt that God will do the same thing with you if you believe in His power! The jars are symbolic of the plan, structure, or blueprint for your life. We must present to God something to bless or to increase because He desires to do so. However, we sometimes are looking for God to give us increase before we have a plan, or before we have created a structure for Him to bless. We must always remember that God is able to do exceedingly, abundantly above all that we could ask or think, but we must do our part in presenting a living sacrifice.

So, the question to you is quite simple. What are you going to present to God today? The idea of forming is to bring together parts or combine to create something. To form means to have a manifestation of something that seems to be irrelevant, but soon will embody something great or relevant. I believe that you have the next great idea, invention, ministry, or business that only you can produce with the help of God. There has always been an urge within you that says, "I am better than this", and I am encouraging you right now to move toward your better days.

There is nothing that you cannot do if you put your mind to it! Begin to form whatever it is that you have been given, and watch God fill it with more resources and finances that will take you to places that you could have never imagined. The Bible says in First Corinthians 2:9; "But as it is written: "Eye hath not seen, nor ear heard, neither have entered into the heart of man the things which God hath prepared for them that love Him."

In closing, the widow in the story continued to bring the jars before the Lord which allowed Him to fill it. Once she stopped bringing jars before the Lord, He ceased from filling them. This is particularly important to understand because the principle is that God fills whatever we present to Him formed. Clearly, God desires to bless His children in a mighty way that will help them to be prosperous both financially and physically. God desires to give you increase in every area of your life so that you may be a blessing to others in His Name. The widow in Second Kings chapter 4 was broken in the beginning of the story, but as she was obedient to the command that was given to her to get jars, she received increase. As a result, in verse seven of Second Kings she was instructed to Go, sell the oil and pay her debts which will allow her and her sons to live. I believe that we must realize that God wants us to live, and to enjoy life while being obedient to His commands. Therefore, let us learn a lesson from the widow, and present to God our plans and watch Him bless it abundantly! There is nothing too hard for God, and there is no problem too difficult for Him.

Chapter 6:

Living My Best Life

The challenge that many of us face is that we are not prepared to embrace the life that we can have because in our minds it seems impossible to grasp. Who are you to be wealthy, famous, or prosperous in all areas of your lives? Who are you to be the lender and not the borrower, or to be the head and not the tail? A fellow author, Marianne Williamson states, "Our deepest fear is not that we are inadequate. Our deepest fear is that we are powerful beyond measure. It is our light, not our darkness that most frightens us. We ask ourselves, 'Who am I to be brilliant, gorgeous, talented, or fabulous?' Who are you not to be? You are a child of God. Your playing small does not serve the world. There is nothing enlightened about shrinking so that other people will not feel insecure around you. We are all meant to shine, as children do. We are born to make manifest the glory of God that is within us. It is not just in some of us; it is in everyone. And as we let our own light shine, we unconsciously give other people permission to do the same.

As we are liberated from our own fear, our presence automatically liberates others." There must be a desire within us that encourages us to go forward with our ideas and live the life that expresses the greatness that we have within. Therefore, the life that we live must be lived to the best of our ability. Imagine if you did not have any financial restrictions, any social barriers, any health issues, or anything preventing you from living your best life today. What would you be doing? The answer to that question should be the answer that shows you if you are living your best life, or not. It should help you to find out if you are living for the moment or living for the excitement that should come with every day of you waking up. I believe that many of us have been living our lives to not make a mistake, rather than to enjoy the risk that we must take to create a memorable experience. One of my favorite movies, The Last Holiday starring Queen Latifah speaks about the fact that we can sometimes miss out on the greater things in life because we are afraid of the unknown.

In that movie, Queen Latifah whose character's name was Georgia Byrd from New Orleans was an employee in the cookware department in Kragen's Department Store was shy, and unassuming. She recorded in a book called "Possibilities" her dreams of a better life one day. Unfortunately, in the movie when Georgia Byrd hit her head on a kitchen cabinet, she went to get an x-ray to only receive results showing that she has a terminal brain injury and a few days to live. As a result, Georgia Byrd went to her bank and withdrew all the bonds and savings that she had and opened the book of "possibilities". This is interesting because she was living a very conservative life to the degree whereas she never did anything that she dreamed to do up to that point. She thought about it, but she did not move forward with living the life that was better and more enjoyable. It appears her receiving the ill-fated news that she was going to die in a few days prompted her to begin to be more adventurous and live her life to the fullest. As the movie ends, it is revealed that the x-ray machine that tested Georgia Byrd was faulty, therefore, she was the same healthy person before the misdiagnosis but with a new perspective on life. In comparison, we need to make sure that we live our lives to the best of our ability and not wait until we are older or sick to set our minds on accomplishing our goals and aspirations in our lifetime.

Consider climbing that mountain, running with the bulls, or flying across the country to see one of the seven wonders of the world. It is without hesitation that you must seek to live your best life while the blood is running warm in your veins. You must strive to accomplish the things that you have been putting off for so long because of fear and shame. Living your best life is a phrase that means to live to the best of your ability, and to have fun while doing it. We must never make decisions that are not safe or can risk our lives, but we can make decisions that are going to create pleasant memories for years to come.

Chapter 7:

God's Plan or My Plan

The plan of God is often uncomfortable to us because we have our own agenda and our own plan(s) for our lives. I have found out that God will not make you do what your faith has not compelled you to do. He will give you signs, wonders, and allow you to see what could be but you must have faith in Him. Throughout the bible, we have learned that many individuals were blind, deaf, and barren until they displayed faith in God. According to Matthew 13:58, "Now He did not do many mighty works there because of their unbelief." Jesus had the power to move and transform the lives of all those that He encountered, but because of their unbelief, He do not do any mighty works. Imagine for a minute and ask yourself a question regarding your life. Is Jesus holding back His power in my life because I have unbelief? Is there a possibility for me to have more but I am in the way? As you consider these questions, make sure that you investigate your heart with clarity so that you can make the adjustments that are necessary for growth.

What is your plan for your life? What are the next steps and how do you plan on completing them? Many people do not make plans outside of their current situations or environment. Purpose is defined as the reason why something is done or used, the aim or intention of something. Purpose is the feeling of being determined to do or achieve something or the aim or goal of a person. Simply, purpose is what a person is trying to do and/or become. The great motivational speaker, Les Brown says "To sit on an idea or fail to act on a goal is not really goal-setting, but wishful thinking. Wanting something is not enough. You must hunger for it. Your motivation must be absolutely compelling in order to overcome the obstacles that will invariably come your way." We should make plans while ensuring that we are allowing God to direct our steps toward a purpose-driven life.

As you have read, the title presents a choice between God's plan or my plan. Quite naturally, many of you may be familiar with the song entitled God's plan. This rap song spoke primarily about the fact that many times things that happen in our lives are seen by others as a struggle and/ or a tragedy.

People may see the tough times that we may be having but at the end of the day, it is all in God's Hands. It is through the power of God which may seem detrimental in other's eyes but was simply a period of growth for greater. According to the Bible, God does have a plan for your life and a reason for all the things that you may be going through at this time. Scripture declares in Jeremiah 29:11; "For I know the plans I have for you," declares the Lord, "plans to prosper you and not to harm you, plans to give you hope and a future." Let us look at this verse in its context. After the Jews are placed into captivity by the Babylonian empire, and the prophets both in Jerusalem and in Babylon were proclaiming the imminent ending of the exile near 595/4 BC (before Christ). As previously promised by Jeremiah, the captivity in Babylon would not go beyond seventy years. It is now in this text that God has appointed an end to it, but it would be a long season in exile before God would cause them to return to the place called home. False prophets promised a quick return from exile even though the Lord told them through Jeremiah that it would not be a quick return, but there would be a return. God speaks through the prophet Jeremiah in verse 11 but reassuring them that he has a plan and a purpose for their current circumstance. Parenthetically, you must know that God has a plan and a purpose for your life too!

God knew His own thoughts toward these exiled Jews in Babylon, and He knew that they would come out of their current bondage. It was through the power of God that they would have a future of hope and not one of despair. We must continue to remind ourselves that God has a plan for our lives! He desires to use you for His glory and His honor. The prophet Jeremiah communicates a message of hope by reminding them that God thinks about them and that He has better for them. The exiled Jews lived in experience of God's judgment upon their nation. Consequently, they could have felt that because God has allowed us to be in bondage that He does not care about our well-being. So, Jeremiah whose name means, "Yahweh will exalt" or "God will exalt" tells them that amid their temporary calamity that they would be delivered. Therefore, Jeremiah states that God will give them a future and hope which is exactly what God's plan is for your life. Consider how awesome God is and how He delivers us from our fears and faults. God's plan is always a work that is in progress, and He is always pruning us so that we may be ready to fulfill the destiny that is on our lives.

We can tend to lean upon our own understanding regarding the direction for our lives because we do not know our purpose. Therefore, I would like to give you a little more direction on making sure that you align your purpose with God's plan. The apostle Paul writes in Ephesians 2:10; "For we are His workmanship, created in Christ Jesus unto good works, which God hath before ordained that we should walk in them." The apostle Paul states that we are being worked on by God, and that we must embrace the idea that our purpose is to do good works. God's plan is for us to do good works while we live. We must do good works which is defined as acts of charity, kindness, or good will. This expression, also put as **good** work, originally had the theological **meaning** of an act of piety. The comfort in knowing that when we do good works that God is pleased is a mighty blessing! Second Corinthians 5:10 states that "For we must all appear before the judgment seat of Christ, that each one may receive the things done in the body, according

47

to what he has done, whether good or bad." Our plans are oftentimes driven by the flesh and the cares of this the world. The world meaning the systems and the thoughts that go against the Word of God. First John 2 verse 16 states, "For all that is in the world—the lust of the flesh, the lust of the eyes, and the pride of life—is not of the Father but is of the world." So, may me evaluate our plans and find out what is the driving force behind them. If they are driven by selfishness, money, and/ or manipulation, you must not succumb to your plans. On the other hand, if they are driven by love, compassion, and generosity then you should move forward in prayer.

In conclusion, the reality is that God's plan must be our plan, and our plan must be God's plan. I am hopeful that we all can love God throughout our lives and allow Him to show us the way!

What Is Your Plan?

Scripture References for Planning:

Proverbs 21:5

The plans of the diligent lead surely to abundance, but everyone who is hasty comes only to poverty.

Luke 14:28

"For which of you, desiring to build a tower, does not first sit down and count the cost, whether he has enough to complete it?"

Proverbs 16:3

Commit your work to the Lord, and your plans will be established.

Jeremiah 29:11

"For I know the plans I have for you," declares the Lord, "plans for welfare and not for evil, to give you a future and a hope."

Proverbs 19:21

Many are the plans in the mind of a man, but it is the purpose of the Lord that will stand.

1 Corinthians 14:12

So with yourselves, since you are eager for manifestations of the Spirit, strive to excel in building up the church.

1 Corinthians 14:40

But all things should be done decently and in order.

1 Timothy 4:7

Have nothing to do with irreverent, silly myths. Rather train yourself for godliness.

Amos 3:7

For the Lord God does nothing without revealing his secret to his servants the prophets.

Ecclesiastes 3:1

For everything there is a season, and a time for every matter under heaven.

Isaiah 28:29

This also comes from the Lord of hosts; he is wonderful in counsel and excellent in wisdom.

Isaiah 32:8

But he who is noble plans noble things, and on noble things he stands.

Isaiah 55:8

"For my thoughts are not your thoughts, neither are your ways my ways," declares the Lord.

Isaiah 55:9

"For as the heavens are higher than the earth, so are my ways higher than your ways and my thoughts than your thoughts."

Matthew 6:34

"Therefore do not be anxious about tomorrow, for tomorrow will be anxious for itself. Sufficient for the day is its own trouble."

Philippians 4:6

Do not be anxious about anything, but in everything by prayer and supplication with thanksgiving let your requests be made known to God.

Proverbs 11:14

Where there is no guidance, a people falls, but in an abundance of counselors there is safety.

Proverbs 13:16

In everything the prudent acts with knowledge, but a fool flaunts his folly.

Proverbs 15:22

Without counsel plans fail, but with many advisers they succeed.

Proverbs 16:1

The plans of the heart belong to man, but the answer of the tongue is from the Lord.

Proverbs 16:9

The heart of man plans his way, but the Lord establishes his steps.

Proverbs 19:2

Desire without knowledge is not good, and whoever makes haste with his feet misses his way.

Proverbs 20:18

Plans are established by counsel; by wise guidance wage war.

Proverbs 21:20

Precious treasure and oil are in a wise man's dwelling, but a foolish man devours it.

Proverbs 23:4

Do not toil to acquire wealth; be discerning enough to desist

LIFE PRINCIPLES FOR FULFILLING YOUR PURPOSE

Life Principle #1

Everyone Cannot Stay

While you are growing, remember that everyone in your life is not meant to stay forever. There are things and people in your life that are there to either teach you, help you, or hurt you. Some people are in your life to teach you how to grow and how to be able to make it to the next level in your life. For example, when I was growing up, I met a lot of young men my age because I played basketball in my community. It was during that time in my life that I met a young man that later became my best friend, Keon Thomas. Keon lived a few houses down from my house growing up, and we became close friends. As teenagers, Keon would always challenge me in basketball, football, ping-pong, and even running. He was a very athletic person and was almost great at everything he played. Around our final year in high school, my friend for over five years had begun to hang out with a different crowd which cause him to stay up all night, and to get in trouble almost daily. Although he began hanging around a negative crowd, I still occasionally spoke to him throughout the week.

Around this same time, I began feeling the calling that God had on my life to minister and counsel those that were spiritually defeated. I noticed that although Keon was my dear friend, it was evident that our relationship was beginning to change and that we were heading in two different directions in our lives. Later that year, Keon got arrested and was now in prison for a serious crime. Even though I loved Keon, and he was my best friend, I realized that he was in my life for just a season. He was not meant to stay forever, but he was someone that God was using to teach me how to always try my best, and to learn how to walk away from the wrong environment. I appreciate Keon, and I am happy that he was in my life, and although he is currently still in prison, I am praying for him every day! We must realize that it is okay to grow up into a more mature version of yourself which will automatically cause change in your life.

Everyone is not meant to stay forever, and we must be wise enough to be good students while we are being taught by life. There are some individuals that are in your life for a season to help you with recognizing the areas in your life that are needed for growth. We must continue to grow into our true selves daily and continue to prune the things in our lives that seem to be holding us back from reaching our destiny. Someone once said, "The first step towards getting somewhere is to decide that you are not going to stay where you are." There will be seasons in your life that you will be alone, and there will be seasons in your life when you have an abundance of friends but remember that it is just a season! Dr. Martin Luther King, Jr. once stated, "If you can't fly then run, if you can't run then walk, if you can't walk then crawl, but whatever you do you have to keep moving forward." It is the ability to move forward that allowed me to appreciate the friends that I had while embracing the friends that are to come. On the other hand, as a pastor I have seen individuals come to the house of God and stated in front of the church that they are ready to commit. They may have just experienced a death of a loved one, or recently loss their job, or had fallen on hard times in life. Consequently, they decide to come to the Lord, which is the right thing to do, but their surrender was not for their lifetime, it was just for a moment.

Witnessing this as a pastor has given me the knowledge to know that everyone will not stay, but they are either there for the tragedy, triumph, or the trepidations. It is my belief that people come to God because of **TRAGEDY** knowing that God is loving and that through His Word there is healing. People come to the Lord because of **TRIUMPH** because they have recently gotten married or have finally been hired for the job they always wanted. Lastly, they come to the Lord because of **TREPIDATIONS** meaning having feelings of anxiety or fear. During times of trepidations, there is a vulnerability that occurs within, and many people serve the Lord during these times in their lives until they feel better. Whether it is tragedy, triumph, or trepidations many have not stayed consistently to serve the Lord. Therefore, we must not fret or become discouraged over those that do not stay but we must keep our eyes focused on our purpose and our God. By doing this, you will continue to shine in the dark places, and you will stand strong amid every circumstance.

The purpose of life is a life of purpose.

— Robert Byrne

Life Principle #2

Get Over It

Sometimes you will become bothered by the pressures of life that seem to weigh you down. Life can become so overwhelming to the degree that you are unable to fulfill your goals in life. The term "get over it" means to not allow the past to ruin your life or stop you from moving ahead in life. I have realized that if you are alive, there will always be problems and situations that will occur. Therefore, you must embrace the situation whenever it comes your way and deal with it while moving forward! Some of the greatest individuals that have ever lived have faced adversity, and they have been able to properly navigate through it all to obtain success. I am learning every day that when you are busy working on improving yourself, there will be haters, manipulators, and people that do not want you to be great. There will be people in your own family that will become jealous of your growth and development. People from your neighborhood growing up will possibly despise you because you had the audacity to move out of the neighborhood and choose to live in a more comfortable place. Knowing all these things, you must learn to develop the mindset to get over it. The resilience to not allow negative commentary to cause you to become discouraged to cease from growing as an individual is what will carry you through.

We must realize that we are not meant to be on the same level forever. Consider the butterfly and moth and how they develop through a process called metamorphosis. The Greek word for metamorphosis means transformation or change in shape. Butterflies, moths, beetles, flies, and bees have complete metamorphosis. According to the academy of natural sciences of Drexel University, there are four stages in metamorphosis of butterflies and moths: egg, larva, pupa, and adult. The first stage which is the egg stage is the time where the egg is laid on plants by the adult female butterfly with the intention for the egg to make the plant its food. Next, the larva stage which is essentially the caterpillar if the insect is a butterfly or moth. During this time, the caterpillar's sole job is to eat abundantly, and as it grows the caterpillar sheds skin because it grows almost 100 times its size during this stage. Then, the transition stage as it is affectionally called, the caterpillar becomes a pupa or chrysalis. This stage is when depending on the species that it is suspended under a branch, hidden in leaves or buried underground. In the case of a caterpillar, it would be inside a cocoon of silk which is keeping it protected from the outside elements.

I really like this stage because it may look like nothing is going on outwardly but there are big changes happening on the inside. The special cells that were present in the larva are now growing rapidly such as the legs, wings, eyes, and other parts of the adult butterfly. Lastly, the reproductive stage or the adult stage is when the butterfly appears, and the beauty of growth is on full display. The caterpillar's job was to eat, and now the adult's job is to mate and lay eggs. The butterfly sores throughout the forest or garden as a beauty to behold like none other. If you did not know that the butterfly went through a metamorphosis, you could not properly appreciate its beauty at this stage of its life. You may be in one of the stages of metamorphosis in your life now, and it can be difficult to appreciate the process, but I want you to stay strong! Your courage to press forward will allow you to develop the beauty that will be on display for everyone to see very soon. The butterfly soars through the wind, stands tall on every branch, and when others see it, they are utterly amazed. Remember, for you to grow into the person that you can truly be, you must learn to "get over it." You can do it!!

A noble purpose inspires sacrifice, stimulates innovation and encourages perseverance.

— Gary Hamel

Life Principle # 3

Each One, Teach One

This phrase originated in the United States during slavery, when Africans were denied education, including learning to read. Many if not most enslaved people were kept in a state of ignorance about anything beyond their immediate circumstances which were under control of owners, the lawmakers and authorities. When an enslaved person learned or was taught to read, it became their duty to teach someone else, spawning the phrase "Each one, teach one."

Personally, I am the product of someone taking time to teach me about life, and how to become the priest, provider, and protector of my family. It was through their investment in me that I was also able to grow to appreciate integrity and have respect for all of mankind. Too many times we witness people treating each other harshly, and reluctant to help those in need. It is particularly important to help those that need your knowledge, wisdom, power, and even your time because one day you may need help too. By the grace of God, He allowed you to make it to the level where you are financially, physically, emotionally, and intellectually advanced. Therefore, you must reach back to succor your fellow brother and sister to get to the levels in which you have already reached. We must realize that success is not making large amounts of money or living in the biggest house. Success is helping those that are in need and assisting them to become the best version of themselves daily. Why do we have such a difficult time seeing others advance in their lives? Why is it that we become so jealous when we hear about someone that looks like us move from one level to the next? We must realize that there is enough room at the table for all of us, and we should not feel inferior because others are prospering.

According to Psychology Today in an article written by Robert L. Leahy, Ph.D., "Why it doesn't feel good when someone else succeeds." It states that you find yourself thinking that they do not deserve this or that they think they are superior to me. According to the article, it states that we begin to reflect on how inferior we are and believe that people start looking at us as a loser. We tend to envy people with whom we compare ourselves with such as a colleague, a sibling, a classmate, and one of our in-laws. We envy achievements that we think are possibilities for us – but we do not feel confident in achieving them. For example, you might not envy someone who wins the Nobel Prize, because they are out of your league, but you do envy a classmate who got promoted in your shared field. We are more likely to envy someone when we think that their advantage is not deserved, since our envy often carries with it the sense of injustice. Envy often leads us to become depressed, anxious, and angry. We dwell on the unfairness or our sense of futility. We complain to other people about this – perhaps alienating them envious. We may even give up competing altogether, because we think that it just reminds us of our sense of failure or our belief that we cannot stand the unfairness.

As mentioned, there can be a lot of emotions and reactions that can occur when others advance in a perspective field and we may not. Nevertheless, it is still crucial if you are the one that has been advanced or has achieved certain things to help others. To give them an extended hand by rendering knowledge, labor, or mentorship so that we all can grow together.

According to Wikipedia.org, the United States of America has a financial position which includes assets of at least $269.6 trillion and debts of $145.8 trillion to produce a net worth of $123.8 trillion as of Q1 2014. So, you can truly obtain whatever you desire and still help another person to reach their goal as well. There is no harm in helping someone from behind to get a boost from you. I remember watching football the other day, and the same player that tackled the quarterback was the same player that reached his hand down to lift him back up again. In the sports world, this is called sportsmanship which is defined as fair and generous behavior or treatment of others, especially in a sports contest. The athlete that displays good sportsmanship is the one that has been on the receiving side of the lost, but still takes out time to tell the winner good game. Unfortunately, everyone is not willing to display fairness and generosity in sports, but those that are will always be blessed!

Consider someone that you may know that has been trying to launch their own brand, make a product, get their business started, or simply become a better person. The person that comes to mind should receive a call from you with an encouraging word, and an offer to assist them in their growth. By doing this, you have demonstrated the great characteristic of humility and love that helps our world be better. There is always room for others at the proverbial table! Regardless of if you have achieved greatness already, or you are on your way to becoming great, always remember to help someone in the process. Each one **MUST** teach one!

Find out who you are. And do it on purpose.

— Dolly Parton

Life Principle # 4

Trust the Process!

I must admit, life is exceedingly difficult to live when you start at the bottom of the barrel. It can truly bring its challenges with it and if you are not careful, you will give up on it. There are many people that I know that have faced challenges throughout their lives such as losing their mother to death at an early age, or not knowing whom their biological father is. Some people have dealt with troubling situations early in life nevertheless they have been able to persevere through it all. The have been able to endure the toils and troubles of life by developing strength that allows them to never lose sight of the victory ahead. It has been my hope and desire to be like so many people that can take a hit and still stand strong! This life principle is one that has difficulty because it communicates the fact that there is not any instant gratification, whereas one must work towards it to obtain the prize.

The word process means a series of actions or steps taken in order to achieve a particular end. The goal is to bring to reality your vision that you have set out to accomplish. As you continue to pursue your purpose, remember that there are steps and procedures that must be taken to get to the place where you desire to be. Knowing this, you must first start at the beginning! Sometimes we wrestle within ourselves because we have not achieved the goals that we wanted to achieve in the time period in which we desire to. Be not dismayed, the key is to start at the beginning. You must take the first step which could be doing one push up, drinking one cup of water, reading one page at a time, making one sale, or attending one event. By simply just starting, you can begin to create a routine that will gradually bring you to your goal and vision for your life.

Next, you must expect as you begin to get smarter, stronger, and wiser that there will be those that will not support you in any facet of your progression. While you are growing feed on the negativity and animosity that may come your way and use it as you get to your goal. There will be people that will stop believing in you, and even tell you that you do not have enough to achieve your goal but trust the process. Thomas Edison, the inventor of the light bulb failed one thousand times before inventing the light bulb. During an interview, a reporter jokingly asked him, "How did you feel to fail one thousand times?" To which Edison replied, "I didn't fail one thousand times. The light bulb was an invention with one thousand steps." The main point that Thomas Edison was trying to convey to the reporter was that there is a process for every achievement whether small or great. There are many things that you may have started but somehow you managed to either momentarily quit or give up all together. Even though you may have quit or given up, it is never too late to start over again today!

Growing up I always knew that God had called me to be a minister or someone that helps people become greater after counseling with me. It has always been in me to help people and encourage them from the inside out either through preaching, counseling, mentoring, or through teaching. Knowing this, I struggled to find out how God would use me to do this, and why is He calling me? After years in my teenage years wrestling with being used by God, I finally surrendered at my senior year of high school in two thousand and one. In began to watch my grandfather and others teach the word of God in a mighty way and began to learn by following before I could lead. Although I occasionally stumbled in my learning and growing, my grandfather always encouraged me to never give up and keep my eye on the power of God in my life!

From the age of 15 years old to 28 years old, my grandfather taught me how to minister with a "velvet hammer" approach. I was willing to follow before I could lead knowing that there was a process to achieve greatness. On August 2011, I was installed as the Senior Minister of the Brownsville Church of Christ and I was prayed over by over ten ministers and preachers of the gospel of Christ. Many young men today preach one sermon, and now they want to be the leader of the whole congregation. They do not desire to follow anyone or take the time to be taught by anyone. They repudiate the process, and as a result they are not rooted and grounded in the truth. The process of growing is necessary, and it should be embraced so that when tough times arise within your business, ministry, or in your personal life you will have the capacity to withstand the obstacles. The process is the most important part of the journey so appreciate it while you have it. May you make it through the steps and conquer the things that you have set out to accomplish.

The secret of success is constancy to purpose.

— Benjamin Disraeli

Life Principle #5

Move in Silence!

The devil is busy! The Bible states in John 10:10; The thief does not come except to steal, and to kill, and to destroy. I have come that they may have life, and that they may have it abundantly. Clearly, God desires for us to have abundance in our lives. Nevertheless, the thief which is scripturally symbolic of the devil desires to kill, steal, and destroy our abundance that God desires for our lives. Therefore, it has become my practice to move in silence and to make sure that I am being very strategic regarding who I tell my plans to. I realized that everyone around you is not always happy about your pursuit of happiness and financial freedom. There are people that are content with you being on the same level as them financially, intellectually, relationally, and spiritually.

Furthermore, if you do not create, build, or grow those kinds of people will be by your side every step of the way. However, if you begin to create, build, and grow you will find that the same people will leave you because you dared to want more for yourself and your family. Therefore, you must move in silence which is a process of waiting patiently for the manifestation to come forth, pursuing purpose with due diligence. It consists of putting in the work and fulfilling the tasks at hand without seeking external validation from your peers or calling attention to you while you do the work. There is a strength that occurs when a person is focused on their goals and aspirations for their life while not worrying about what other people are doing.

There are a lot of people in this world that like to publicize the things that they are doing for the purpose of getting affirmation from others. Sometimes people post pictures on social media of them giving food to a homeless person under the bridge, or how they are building a business. It is my belief that our intentions of our publicizing our endeavors our extremely important, meaning are we doing it for "likes" or for encouragement? Therefore, it is oftentimes important to move in silence so that you can be great without distraction and discouragement. It is in the ability to work without distraction that you can plan accordingly, work based upon your schedule, and create your own limitations for your project reveal. You must know that God has placed things on your heart and in your mind to present to the world one day. You have the talent and the vision to be whatever it is that you believe that you can be. Therefore, never allow yourself to feel tempted to brag, boast, or speak loudly about what your next steps may be. You are great, and even though individuals around you may not see your greatness today, be not dismayed because God will exalt you in due time!

Faith is taking the first step even when you cannot see the whole staircase.

— Martin Luther King Jr.

Life Principle #6

Settle the Business Before the Creativity

While you begin to walk in your purpose and fulfill the goals that you have set forth for your life, remember to take care of the business before you share any idea. Many times, you may be extremely excited about sharing your new ideas of how you have created a new product or how you are about to open another business. You may begin to ask for people to help you bring your vision to fruition to do something great. It is wise to make sure that you take care of the business side before the creativity and vision casting. To take care of the business side means to discuss money, exit clause, everyone's salary, and the terms of each contract with all individuals. This phase of the process is extremely important because when you begin to start telling people your vision and share with them your success plan, things can become strange amazingly fast. For example, there may be someone in your family that is an incredibly good artist and can create your logo for your company. If the business is not discussed before you share the logo idea, or your family member fails to discuss their compensation for creating the logo, it can become a problem.

A problem can arise because each person is going off an assumption that because you are my family member that you will create a logo pro-bono. Or, although you are my family member, I have a price for my services. As a result, a problem may occur because neither person effectively communicated before work started to be done. This example happens a lot within families and friends that no longer are speaking because they did something for a price, but they were not paid because they were considered family. This life principle will save you a lot of stress and legal fees when you take time to discuss the terms of a persons' services, so that before any ideas began to be presented, everyone knows where they stand. Many people fall victim to sharing their intellectual property with people that are back stabbers, manipulators in business, and who will listen to your idea then copyright it before you do.

Remember, doing business can be gruesome at times but it is necessary! You must make sure that you have the expectations of the business relationship set before you move forward with your project or invention. It is a guarantee that people will start off feeling excited to work with you, they will become so happy to be on your team. However, when they one day become upset in the relationship, it becomes imperative that you have already discussed the terms of exit within the contract. The problem that I have observed since my time of doing business is that many people do not possess the ability to separate a personal relationship from a professional relationship. Sometimes people believe that because you are close with them or that they know you personally that whatever you both do relating to business that it is free. Furthermore, they would seem to get offended when you ask them to sign a contract or begin to discuss with them the fees for your services. John D. Rockefeller Sr. an American business magnate and philanthropist states, "a friendship built on business can be glorious, while a business built on friendship can be murder."

Thore are ideas that we all come up with throughout the day that can be very prosperous for us, but we must be strategic on who we present these ideas to, and when. It is without a doubt that you are going to need help to develop your ideas into a profit, but just be careful how you do it. I understand that we live in a manipulating society, and if you do not know what you need to do to be successful, no one will tell you. Therefore, keep in mind that God gave you the idea, so handle it with care. If you settle the business before the creativity, you will be successful and legally covered.

You cannot embrace your destiny if you do not let go of your history.

— T. D. Jakes

Life Principle #7

Tomorrow will be Better

In order to be great, you must realize that failure will happen. It is inevitable that you will at times make the wrong decisions, trust the wrong people, make a bad deal that perhaps will cause you to feel inadequate. Fret not! There is a brighter day tomorrow, and you will have another chance to try it over again. We must realize that greatness must be able to endure the difficult stages towards its development. It may seem like your change has not come, and that it may never come. Life has seemingly been difficult for you and you may be now on the verge of giving up. Well, before you give up or quit, wait until tomorrow to see what will happen. Perhaps your relationship, finances, or your health seems to not be getting any better, I want to encourage you to wait until tomorrow. Tomorrow is a brand-new day and full of new opportunities that are waiting for you to give a chance to. Sometimes we try to accomplish everything in one day, as a result we become disappointed with our progress and in the process. The Bible reminds us in Galatians 6:9; "So let us not get tired of doing what is good. At just the right time we will reap a harvest of blessing if we do not give up." (NLT) I realize that sometimes you can put so much effort into producing the best product or presentation, but the reaction that you hoped for is not what occurs. Furthermore, you could have spent a ton of money to ensure that things work out in your favor, but unfortunately something happened that caused you to not accomplish your goals. Maybe it was a rain delay that caused the event you were hosting to be cancelled, or the venue that you paid for has incurred an issue and you are unable to get your money back. Regardless, remember that tomorrow will be a better day!

I recall when I first began to preach, and my grandfather would continue to encourage me to look on the bright side of things. I would, and still occasionally mess up on my delivery of the Word of God by mispronouncing words, shouting when I should be whispering, or looking down when I should be looking up. My grandfather would tell me to keep my head up, never give up, and that tomorrow will be a better day. I would get discouraged because when I would preach, the church members did not always say "amen" when I expected them to say it. Or that they would not all shake my hand when I was standing at the exit after worship service had concluded in the sanctuary. Things like that would sometimes cause me to become discouraged and sad, but my grandfather would tell me that tomorrow will be a better day. Therefore, I am reminding you that tomorrow will be a better day, and even though today was not your best day, things will get better. As you work on improving your processes and making yourself great in every area of your life, keep your head up because your CHANGE is coming. The Bible says in Proverbs 6:6-8; "Go to the ant, thou sluggard; consider her ways, and be wise: Which having no guide, overseer, or ruler, provides her meat in the summer, and gathered her food in the harvest." (KJV) The ant continues in her ways without having a guide or an overseer, she continues to be one that perseveres through all seasons in her life. As a result, she has the things that she made up in her mind to work for, knowing that tomorrow will be a better day!

*Too many of us
are not living our
dreams because
we are living our
fears.*

— Les Brown

Life Principle # 8

Seek the Kingdom First

This principle can be found in Matthew 6:33 of God's written Word. Throughout your life of success, you must remember to always seek the Kingdom of God first. To seek the Kingdom first means to put God's agenda first in our lives while living our lives under His authority. God is very vital to your success, and He is the only one that can make provisions for you in every endeavor in your life. For without Him, you would not have woken up this morning, or would not have been able to make rational decisions. We must never forget that we move, live, and breathe because of the grace of God on our lives. Therefore, you must always seek Him and His Kingdom first regarding your time, talents, and your treasures. Whenever you are planning your day or adding things to your calendar, remember that God must be first in your planning. For example, if you are planning a trip out of town or on a cruise, make sure that you set a designated time to worship God and thank Him for the blessings that He has given to you. Many times, people tend to overlook God in their planning for their life aspirations. Sure, a person may say a prayer or give an offering when it is convenient, but the consistency of seeking the Kingdom of God first is not apparent. In order to have sustainability in this world, and to be pleasing in God's sight you must be faithful and consistent.

We must remember that everything belongs to God! The Bible says in Psalms 24: 1 – 2; "The earth is the Lord's, and the fullness thereof; the world, and they that dwell therein. For He hath founded it upon the seas, and established it upon the floods..." The Lord God is the creator and the sustainer of it all, He has given each of us a portion to be good stewards which is to be a good manager. Therefore, each of us should strive to remember Him in all that we receive by making sure we give to the Kingdom of God before we do anything else. This principle has allowed billionaires and the wealthy to continue to have sustainability because they have developed a system of reciprocity.

What is the Kingdom of God? It is the sovereign rule of God that consist of His agenda and His authority as King. He is the one that has the control and thereby encourages those that are believers to walk under His authority and operate our lives according to His agenda. Therefore, when we are encouraged to seek first the Kingdom of God, we are asked to put his will and way before ours so that He may be glorified. There are individuals that have struggled with this life principle because they do not fully comprehend the power of God in their lives and how He can bless them abundantly. Furthermore, many have struggled in this area because they may be caught up with the cares of this world along with its temptations. We must seek God first, and never lose sight that He is able to keep us, direct us, and bless us in a mighty way.

The future depends on what you do today.

— Mahatma Gandhi

Life Principle # 9

Watch your connections!

The bible states in First Corinthians chapter 15 and verse 33, "Do not be misled: Bad company corrupts good character." (NIV) In other words, be careful whom you are connected to because they can cause you to make unwise decisions. Depending upon whom you allow yourself to hang around with, associate yourself with, or talk to daily, you must know that it can profoundly affect you in a variety of ways. A wise man once said, "A man only learns in two ways, one by reading, and the other by association with smarter people." Think about the electrical system and how it has a lot of safeguards against danger from bad wire connections. In order to know if you have a bad connection, it is advised to plug a light into a dead outlet on the circuit and turn it on. Have someone watch the light while you remove the cover of the live outlet or switch and wiggle it with a wooden stick. If the light flickers, there is probably a loose connection in the outlet or switch. This example can easily apply to your daily lives when it comes to evaluating your connections and associations.

In comparison to an electrical example, you must remove the cover or look introspectively and investigate the reason why it is always dark or cloudy in your life. Who are you connected to? Is that person(s) helping me to be a better person? What are the benefits of our relationship? I believe that these questions when they are asked honestly will allow anyone to have clarity on where the bad connection is in their lives. On another note, a person can sometimes allow their mind, time, and energy to be devoted to certain things that unknowingly may have a great influence on them. Such as, music, entertainment, television, social media, and even the books that they read. These things may assist with developing our minds causing us to make the right or wrong decisions daily because of what we have exposed our minds to. Furthermore, you must realize that connections are constantly pulling and feeding off your energy and your interest which can literally affect you financially, emotionally, and spiritually. Depending on your connection you may spend more money rather than save or invest, or you may find yourself crying all the time because of another disappointment by someone you are connected to. Or you may cease praying or attending the house of worship because of the connection that you have to someone or something. I remember hearing someone say that if you are the smartest one out of all your friends, it may be time to find more friends. Whether this is true or not, the bottom line is that you need to watch out for bad connections that are not beneficial for your growth.

Well, what does a good connection look like? A good connection and/ or association is defined as a relationship that is of a true partnership in every way. Also, it is defined as a relationship where both parties are interdependent on each other while assisting each other with maturing daily. A good connection and/ or association is something that does not have jealousy, envy, animosity, or betrayal because each person is genuinely happy when someone succeeds in life. Throughout the years, I have tried to connect with people that will assist me in my growth as a man, father, and preacher of the Gospel of Jesus Christ. I have learned that having the right connections can help you to overcome some barriers that otherwise you would have had a hard time with. One of my preaching friends called me the other day and he encouraged me to keep up the good work in my ministry and to know that he has my proverbial "back" if I ever need him. I was profoundly grateful for his call and to know that he cares for my development as a gospel preacher and as a man.

Once, I heard someone say, "surround yourself around winners so when you win it do not sound like you are bragging." You must be willing to expand your reach and strive to learn from individuals that may know more about a particular subject than you do, and they are not afraid to share it with you. You must strive to learn from individuals that may not look like you, dress like you, or may not be from your neighborhood. Be willing to express where you need help at, or what you are trying to accomplish in life with prayer and God will direct you to the right connection.

Lastly, the bible says in Second Corinthians chapter 6 and verse 14; "Do not be unequally yoked together with unbelievers. For what fellowship has righteousness with lawlessness? And what communion has light with darkness?" The objective in this text from the apostle Paul was written to remind the Corinthians about being influenced by a possible evil environment. He cautions them to not be influenced in their thinking, and to not be conformed to this world but be transformed by the renewing of your mind (Romans 12:2). In this text, he speaks especially to the issue of influence and how there must be a focus on being the positive influence and not succumbing to any negative influences. He is not expressing that we should stay away from those that maybe ungodly. He was writing to remind us to not allow ourselves to be deceived believing that we are strong enough to ward off all ungodly things, but that we must be careful and prayerful. Look around and examine who you are connected to, and who is connected to you? Your connection is your source of energy, innovativeness, strength, and your growth. Who are you texting or talking to daily? You must be strategic regarding who you are connected to, and always make sure that you are putting yourself in the right atmosphere for your growth and development.

The LORD has made everything for its purpose, even the wicked for the day of trouble.

— Proverbs 16:4

Life Principle #10

Maintain Integrity

The question that you must ask yourself is, can I be trusted? Trusted to make the right decision, or to be honest regarding every facet of your life. Trusted to be consistent with being yourself and not conforming to the pressures of society. The ability to maintain integrity throughout adverse situations speaks to the fact that you can handle pressure. Throughout history, there are many that have been unable to maintain their integrity because of temptation from the opposite sex, their desire for money, or their assumption that no one would find out about their lack of integrity. Integrity is the quality of being honest and having strong moral principles, moral uprightness. To maintain integrity means to be honest and to live in accordance with your deepest values in mind. It should be your goal to be consistent so that people can trust you to carry out the things that you stated that you would carry out. I recall witnessing how pastors, leaders, business owners, and even administrators lost their positions and prestige because their character was double-sided. When they were in front of the public eye, they displayed the version of themselves that they believed everyone wanted to see. However, when they were away from the cameras or the masses, their character and values that they spoke about was not consistent with their actions. Robert Brault an American writer states, "You do not wake up one morning a bad person. It happens by a thousand tiny surrenders of self-respect to self-interest."

According to mindtools.com, living a life of integrity means that we never have to spend time or energy questioning ourselves. When we listen to our hearts and do the right thing, life becomes simple. Our life, and our actions, are open for everyone to see, and we do not have to worry about hiding anything. The key to maintaining your integrity is to define your values, analyze every choice you make, and encourage others to have good character. Remember that honesty and integrity are not values that you should live by when it is convenient; they are values that you should live by all the time. I believe that while you are fulfilling your purpose, you are going to be tested to maintain your integrity. Make sure that you are focused on the goal, and do not allow temporary pleasure to cause you a lifetime of disappointment. You have a destiny and a purpose to fulfill while you live, so stay strong my friend and do not allow yourself to fall victim to temptation or manipulation.

Consider King David of the Bible in 2nd Samuel chapter 11 regarding how he failed to operate in good character because of his fleshly desires and assumption that no one was watching his actions. The book of 2nd Samuel chapter 11 begins by stating that the kings are supposed to go out to battle in the spring of the year. However, King David remained in Jerusalem, or in other words he stayed home while others fought on the battlefield. One evening while he was home, he arose from his bed, he went to the roof and saw a beautiful woman bathing whose name was Bathsheba. She was the wife of Uriah the Hittite, a soldier in King David's army that was currently fighting on the battlefield. King David was a man of authority, prestige, and favor so he inquired about the woman and his servants advised him that she was married to one of his soldiers that were fighting on the battlefield. King David did not heed this advisory report and he sent for Bathsheba and slept with her then sent her back home. This story shows how King David allowed his flesh to supersede him making the right decision which should have been to leave Uriah's wife alone. Further into the story when Bathsheba is expecting a child from King David, he sends for her husband Uriah and tries to influence him to sleep with Bathsheba to cover up his transgression.

To King David's surprise, Uriah never goes home, but sleeps at King David's door because he is committed to the battle at hand. He states in 2nd Samuel chapter 11 verse 11, "The ark and Israel and Judah are dwelling in tents, and my lord Joab and the servants of my lord are encamped in the open fields. Shall I then go to my house to eat and drink, and to lie with my wife? As you live, and as your soul lives, I will not do this thing." Uriah refused to sleep with his wife while the other soldiers were on the battlefield. As a result, David sends Uriah to the frontlines of the fight, the place where it is the hottest, and Uriah is killed. King David has allowed himself to become treacherous because he was not able to maintain integrity in this situation. Therefore, he has become an adulterous King, murderer, and deceitful in every shape and form. We must be careful that we do not fall susceptible to the things that King

David fail to, rather we should be focused on being a person of success with integrity.

In conclusion, we should try daily to maintain our integrity throughout every stage of our lives. We are to be sincere in our character while developing ourselves to be an example that others may emulate. The legendary singer Bob Marley states, "The greatness of a man is not in how much wealth he acquires, but in his integrity and his ability to affect those around him positively." My goal is to affect those around me in a positive way so that they may always leave more inspired after interacting with me. There is a great need in our world for people that are focused on doing the right thing, and will not succumb to the pressures of money, sex, fame, or friendships but will maintain integrity.

Many are the plans in a person's heart, but it is the LORD's purpose that prevails.

— Proverbs 19:21

May the Lord bless you; May the Lord keep you; May you allow His face to shine upon you every day of your life. Live your life on purpose and be great in everything that you do!

Min. H.L. Henton

Discussion Questions

Take time to discuss the ideas addressed in this book with your book club or with your group at church. It is imperative that you find your purpose in life while learning from others in the process. Use these discussion questions to create a conversation in any setting.

1. According to the chapter "Smile for the Camera", what are some of the reasons why we may express an outward emotion that we may not feel internally?

_____

_____

_____

_____

_____

_____

2. *What are some of the strategies within this book that you can use to figure out your purpose in life?*

_____

_____

_____

_____

_____

_____

_____

3. *What has been your greatest struggle preventing you from walking in your purpose?*

_____

_____

_____

_____

_____

_____

4. Which life principle for fulfilling your purpose applies to you the most? Which applies to you the least?

_____

_____

_____

_____

_____

_____

5. What are the steps that you plan to take to begin living a purpose-driven life? Write them in chronological order.

_____

_____

_____

_____

_____

_____

6. *What current connections or associations do you need to dissolve? What connections or associations should you be seeking to develop?*

_____

_____

_____

_____

_____

_____

_____

7. *According to the author, why is it important to maintain integrity throughout every stage of your life? What are some things that will attempt to challenge your integrity?*

_____

_____

_____

_____

_____

_____

Made in the USA
Middletown, DE
03 September 2024